# Advance Praise

"Clifford Bernier's *The Silent Art* takes us on a journey through countries, landscapes, musical forms and states of mind. Rivers flow through these places to the beat of conga drums, the wail of an alto sax and the voice of a woman singing scat. To read these poems is to enter a work of expressionist art. We might not always know what we're seeing, and may even find ourselves a bit lost on unfamiliar terrain, yet, in the moments we spend with these poems, we cannot imagine being anywhere else or having any other guide but Bernier. Eventually, our souls catch up with each of these poems, and we are left transformed, knowing a little bit more about this universe than when we started. In that sense, these are ideal poems 'uttered in the ideal way/at the ideal time/ by the ideal/ one.'"

—Judith Valente, correspondent, PBS-TV; co-editor, *Twenty Poems to Nourish Your Soul*; author of *Discovering Moons*

"Like musicians, poets strive for clarity, originality and perfect pitch. Clifford Bernier's *The Silent Art* provides us with a bumper crop of each. As lovers of either genre well know, this is no small achievement. The poems found within this volume consistently walk the very fine lines between lyricism and conviction-detail and surprise. They embody Ezra Pound's directive to those who toil in the poetic vineyard: 'Make It New!' His portraits of John Coltrane and Charles Mingus successfully embody each man's essence, while successfully avoiding the clichés that often torpedo far too many literary portraits of these masters. And while these poems demand our full attention, they are as accessible and as moving as a walk in the forest. Let this music in your life."

—Reuben Jackson

"Clifford Bernier is the consummate performance artist who harmonizes imagery with syncopated language to break through the silence of the page. Make no mistake, *The Silent Art* is a full-blown concert."

—Karren L. Alenier, author of *Gertrude Stein Invents a Jump Early On*

"Clifford Bernier's *The Silent Art* is a beautiful jazz symphony sweetened with the Zen of everydayness and a 'double bass blues for Trane.' Mr. Bernier is a wonderful poet with a musical soul as deep as Mingus. Ah Um indeed. This cat has great chops in the poetry and jazz of life."

—M.L. Liebler, poet and editor of *Working Words: Punching the Clock* and *Kicking Out the Jams*

"Clifford Bernier is a musician of the word... For Bernier wants to 'roll' a 'moon in his mouth & spit it out,' to speak it and play it for the reader in 'syncopated sunsets.' So Charles 'Mingus speaks in Maa,' Ron Carter resolves Sino-Tibetan 'patois' in musical dialects, and John Coltrane 'blows blues,' where sounds of music become meditational ohms immersed in misty and 'rainy nights.' *The Silent Art* is, indeed, composed 'hymns in the transcendent tone of an angel/ probing the harmonic potential of time' and in the space of bistros, clubs and cafés. In the end, Clifford Bernier's *The Silent Art* is music as sung poetry; it is poetry arranged as a concerto. His poetry is 'love, in the furious discovery of spirit/ in the relentless urgency of light' traveling at the speed of sound in the 'appearances' of light waves to be played and heard beyond the eyes of the reader, reading with 'eyes like quarter notes.'"

—Cecilia Martínez-Gil, judge of the Gival Press Poetry Award and author of *Psaltery and Serpentines*

# THE
# SILENT
# ART

## CLIFFORD
## BERNIER

Gival Press

ARLINGTON, VIRGINIA

Published by Gival Press, an imprint of Gival Press, LLC.

For information please write:

Gival Press, LLC

P. O. Box 3812

Arlington, VA 22203

www.givalpress.com

First edition

ISBN 13: 978-1-928589-62-4

eISBN 13: 978-1-928589-68-6

Library of Congress Control Number: 2011934544

Artwork Cover: Copyright © 2011 by Tom Semmes.

Photo of Clifford Bernier by Kyoko Nakamura.

Design by Ken Schellenberg.

# Acknowledgments

Grateful acknowledgment is made to the editors of the publications in which the following poems first appeared, some under different title or in earlier form:

*Alexandria* and *Mount Vernon Gazettes*: "Rainy Night in Old Town"

*Beyond Bones III*: "Overture", "Kyoto", "Moving Pictures", "Appearances"

*Gertrude:* "U Street Strut"

*Gargoyle*: "Congo Square"

*Innisfree Poetry Journal:* "Silk Road Suite", "It Was So Cold I Had to Burn my Poetry to Survive"

*Not Just Air Literary eJournal*: "Dreamtime"

*The Poet's Cookbook:* "Hollerküchle"

*Tuesdays*: "Pax Harmonica"

*Live at IOTA Club & Café (CD):* "Double Bass", "Pax Harmonica", "Rainy Night in Old Town"

*Poetry in Black & White (CD):* "Blues for Trane", "Congo Square", "Intervals"

# For the Musicians

Many of these poems were composed with music in mind. They have been performed in clubs and cafés in the Washington, DC area with the Joshua Carr Group, the Poesis group, and the Villainelles, in multiple variations. Special thanks to Joshua Carr, Andrew Cox, Paul DeCastro, Mike Gillispie, Allen Holmes, Aretha Grayson, James 'Curly' Robinson, and Shep Williams for the inspiration.

# CONTENTS

# OVERTURE

A camera on a tripod

framed two dancers on a screen,

image shimmying and twirling

in 3-inch digital ¡carambá!

as salsa, meringue, and machata

swept the floor. And I thought:

dance, *amigos*, you know how to live,

not stiff and out-of-step like me,


but stay within these words, so I can see you.

# ADAGIO

# THE SILENT ART

i.

In the silent art

ideas plucked from air

arrange the page,

no sound instructs their form.


Consider this page.

Before: nada.

Now: cockatoos.

No choir sang.


Cities are built from illusory walls,

ephemeral passengers ride

translucent trains,

guitars strum wordlessly.


ii.

Cut music from language.

See what remains.

*The Mississippi draining into the Nile.*

*The hypothetical presence of wormholes.*

*Snakes with feet.*

In the silent art, jazz bands
set up without players.
Drums center, keyboard left,
empty mike. Audiences gather, jive.
*The dialectic. The final palm.*

iii.

This page, tossed across silence,
becomes a language.
You study its alphabet.
A street, a tide, a stand of trees.
*Howler monkeys.*

iv.

Yet you cannot speak.

# KYOTO

*i. Inari*

Kitsune, my fox, spread the word.

I am here. I am there.

In the woods I am a snake.

In the village

I am an old man hauling rice.

At this confluence

I am a goat.

Say that each word is a gate,

each step a passage

to a shifting world.


*ii. Shoren-in*

By the dragon bathing in the pond,

a lantern.

A fall, a stone, a maple.

In the composed garden,

moss softens the sculpted boxwoods,

the tended firs.

Carp drift beneath the surface.

Each part is balanced, poised,

a vision of harmony

in a perfect land.

*iii. Sanjusangen-do*

Raijin, storm-god, bring the rain.

Free the thunder, feed the crops.

Fujin, call the wind.

Offer incense, fruit, wine.

Spare my house, my family, my field.

Guard what is given:

See: Peace has eleven faces,

a thousand hands.


*iv. Fushimi*

I am clear. I am dark.

I am a cricket among cicadas.

Above the Kamogawa, the Katsuragawa,

I am a griffin.

Kitsune, turn your key.

Open the granary,

the murmuring trail

beneath the ascending gates.

# Moving Pictures

Set your itinerary.

Chances are
your destination will be there.

Though you are an image, your flight is too.

Or rather,
a frame in a silent movie, flickering.

Not to worry.

Walk its streets,
see its monuments,
meet its people.

You cannot pass through them,
but no sweat.

They are like you, just different.

Lillian Gish birthing a nation.

Charlie Chaplin eating his boot.

*Light reeling the linden tree.*

# LOCATION, LOCATION

*So long and thanks for all the fish.*

*Douglas Adams,* The Hitchhiker's Guide to the Galaxy

*i.*

The blinking world.

What is wrong with this picture?

Follow me.

Let us walk through its silence
as if we were there.

As if koalas did not swing from trees.
As if manatees did not sing.

You are hungry. Feast on roots.

*ii.*

*The road does not release you.*
*The camellia does not compel you.*
*The breeze is not boistered by your pace.*

*iii.*

And yet. To return.

Paris embraces the Seine and raises in its reflection cathedrals of art.

Shanghai rotates like a spaceship from Mars.

Rio and Douala? Sydney and Tehran.

*iv.*

Alpha Centauri?

*Please.*

# ESPRESSIVO

# DREAMTIME

*i*

Under the skin of the earth our ancestors are waiting to be born.


Waiting to be born like the Snake-Man and the Bandicoot,

Cockatoo-Man and the Hawk-Woman soaring,

honeysuckle opening in the billabong,

sun tossed like a stone on a feathered string.

Broken from the shell of an egg,

birds scattered like shards of a rainbow shattered in the dreaming of the First

    Day.



Shattered in the dreaming of the First Day,

as the seed of the earth cracked and the Ancient Ones awakened their eyes

to the light of the stars set like fires in the fields

that warmed the wanderer on his walkabout across the desert that named him.


*Poesis. Water-hole dreaming.*


*And if this were another life, timeless trails would guide my way.*
*If this were another life, a traveler's voice would sing my dreams.*
*If this were another life, her words would move between my words.*

*ii*

Conjured him like the bark of a coolabah tree,

Mother Sun and Lover Moon waxing and waning in the cadence of singing.


Conjured him like ranges raised by the seeker,

tracking notes like footprints of the Ancient Ones who sang before.


Conjured him like the song-map in the rope of stars knotted to the Milky Way,

where he fell like the torch-bearing sun calling for its Spirit-Child,

a mopoke dwelling in his lair.


Conjured him like the drone of a didgeridoo,

crow snatching a fire-stick to slay the snake in the bloodwood tree.


*iii*

She stepped into his dream and sang the verses that named him.

She sang the verses that named him and conjured the land.


She sang him from the sun wandering aimlessly in the sky,

she sang him from the moon teasing the crocodile in the stream.


She sang him from the earth cracking on the First Day,

she sang him from his work and whispered his songs.


She reached for his hand and his eyes became the Southern Cross,

she reached for his legs and his feet became the Southern Sea.

She sang him from the sleep of the Ancestors Dreaming,

she sang him from the stories of Dreamtime.

*And if this were another life, timeless trails would guide my way.*

*If this were another life, a traveler's voice would sing my dreams.*

*If this were another life, her words would move between my words.*

# PAX HARMONICA

Wide as a river that gathers the shoreline
breaking through the thick morning mist.
Banks of the river that guide without borders:
the Yang-tze in Shanghai, the valley of the Rhine.
Draws in the forests, the backroads, the cornfields,
sharecropper shacks in the scratch of the Delta.
Rendered to sound by the whistle of rushes,
black as the soil by the tracks of the Southern,
colored by the Ozarks, the beechwood, the juke joints,
*white-only* signs on the fixtures of fountains.
Wide as a river that gathers the shoreline
breaking through the thick morning mist.

Wide as a river that runs beneath bridges
bordering a great inland sea.
Speaks through the comb of the breeze in the rushes,
draw of the tide in the cluster of marshes,
old-timey tunes in the whistle of reeds.
Crosses the riverbed north of the coastline
to the back-alley bars in the scratch of the Southside;
speaks of the paddle boats steaming from Natchez,
the chromatic flourish of a quartet in Brussels,
avant-garde bistros on the banks of the Seine.
Wide as a river that runs beneath bridges
bordering a great inland sea.

Wide as a river that raises the oceans

voicing the whistle of reeds.

Crosses the border from Shanghai to New Orleans;

travels the county line north of the bayou,

Vicksburg, Greenville, Clarksdale, Memphis,

the progressive bossa of Mauricio in Rio.

Slides in the streets in the scratch of Helena,

blows in the clubs in the clip of Chicago,

follows the Yang-tze from Chongqing to Cathay,

coal towns in Kentucky where the cool water rides.

Wide as a river that raises the oceans

voicing the whistle of reeds.

# CONGO SQUARE

*Beat of a bone on the hide of an ox,*
*entemba, atumpan, conga.*
*Shuffle of feet in the soil of the field:*
*Mandingo, Baoulé, Bakango.*

Plucked like the strings of an mbanza.
Struck like a mamman under the Mapou tree.
Africans abducted and packed into ships
for passage to markets in Haiti, Cuba, Jamaica.
Bound like cargo, sleeping in their waste,
dying from disease and starvation.
Resold to profiteers and auctioned on the block
at Pierre Maspero's Slave Exchange in New Orleans.
Purchased by planters to clear swampland and dig ditches,
haul rocks, assemble shacks,
skilled woodworkers and stonecutters
compelled to pick cotton from sunup to sundown
in heat that burnt the stalks.

But on Sunday, at the far end of town under the live oaks
in the field beyond Rampart Street,
to beating of bones and sticks on drums built from boxes and old pork barrels,

pulsing to slit drums, stool-drums, open-staved drums,

bongos got from gourds and twine,

gutbucket washtubs, bottles filled with teeth,

in a frenzy of leaping rising to madness under the sycamores,

to shrieks of cow-horn hunting crooks,

quill pipes, pan pipes, marimbas cascading

among calls and cries, glides, groans, moans and shouts of Hausa,

Fulani scraping the teeth of a horse's jaw with sticks,

Fanti beating the jaw of an ass with a rusty key,

by Jolof merchant's canvas cast in the dust trading cane,

wearing strange and savage fashions with tails of wild beasts


slaves gathered to remember

making jazz, jaiza, jass, jazz.


At the Place des Nègres in New Orleans

Yorubas drummed the Mamba and the Hougan with the segon and the boula,

tossed cornmeal on the ground, guinea peppers in their mouths

to summon Rada, Gédé, Petro to the Grand Master of Makaya,

as rootman filled the gris-gris with fingernail and powdered brick,

praising stones, plants, snakes, scraps of iron,

Legha, Damballah, Ogou, Zaka.

Lizards and toads, pebbles and shells,

feathers from a chicken breast, hairs from tail of a goat,

graveyard dirt for Santé Dédé

to conjure black cats and roosters for hoodooman

at the orgy in the Bayou St. John on St. John's Eve

to the rhythm of the bone bands

making jazz, jaiza, jass, jazz.


In the pleasure halls and gaming rooms of the Congo

rough men danced with naked women to the raucus presentation

of improvised musical groups of random instrumentation

in a perpetual hedonistic binge with style —

bartenders, cut-throats, cockfighters, thieves,

in Storyville, on Smoky Row,

in the Tenderloin, under the magnolias.

Fanny Sweet, Lulu White, Emma Johnson

and voodoo ladies of the District parlayed tales of the Gumbo Ya-Ya

to patrons of love-oil and goofer dust

with flutes and trumpets fashioned from elephant tusks and rhinoceros horns,

with drums and rattles crafted from calabashes and hollowed-out logs


mulattoes, quadroons, mestizos, octaroons

making jazz, jaiza, jass, jazz,


to the rhythm of the bone bands

making jazz, jaiza, jass, jazz.


*Beat of a bone on the hide of an ox,*

*entemba, atumpan, conga.*

*Shuffle of feet in the soil of the field:*

*Mandingo, Baoulé, Bakango.*

# STACCATO

# AUTUMN 1997

Maddening the 10 years of manic depression

modulating to cadmium in the oak

& ochre elm & the reflection of his regard

in the woods at the window dispersing

his appearance to a clearing &


     a  cobalt sky

          absorbing umber

# WINTER 1998

I know too well the

taut moonlit trees

    before dawn

unearthly shades of

my _____

    hedged pale

absolute in spring

unfolding like knots

silent in winter

      like

# WHISKEY

The fractured moon gleams

    ice in whiskey

splintered against glass

huge & dark

    bare sky at midnight


    one kind of madness

rags bones the rafters

    collision of stars the


       liquid pitch

# PASSAGE

behind the moon a dark coin

purchase of a life

the compassing years


*I want to roll that moon in my mouth*

*& spit it out*


& my car a skiff

a star-crossed tide of traffic

husk of a spent hull


driving the toll road


*the phosphorous wash of the mud wall at Maroua*

*the arc of the path in the desert at dawn*

*the rough bowl of millet wine bought for a quarter*


rub of black wheels &

# ALLEGRO

# DOUBLE BASS

The word in the root at the base of the tree where a man was born,

spoken in Maa:

I love you, *Nakupenda sana.*


In Bantu, Asu, Kiswahili:

Can't wait to see you, *Nameza kukuona tena.*


Deep like a baobab, hard as ebony:

I am here, *Nimestareha sana.*

In Chichewa, Bemba, Fula:

I can speak, *Ninaweza kusema.*


Leaping like antelope on the genetic savannah,

spreading like seed on a hot summer wind,

slapping a pidgin pizzicato to the rhythmic release of a beating heart,

articulating changes to the harmonic structure of the animal,

blowing like vowels on the South China Sea,

assembling like fingerboards in the garrets of Florentine craftsmen,

better than a tuba!

Annobón, Sranan, Tok-Pisin.

Pops Foster, Jimmy Blanton, Charles Mingus:

Mingus Ah Um,

Mingus Ah,

Um.

*Viols as big as myself* claimed Prospero,

tuned in fourths,

inflected like Farsi,

doubled in syntactic symphonies of Niger-Congo and Cushitic families.

Migrating from Dragonetti to Bottesini to Oscar Pettitford.

Afro-Asiatic, Nilo-Saharan, Indo-European,

marking time like petals of an orchid,

branching west like shoots of a palm,

*de latin, en francais, en español, en portugués.*

Schoenberg, Strauss, Stravinsky,

Slam Stewart, Paul Chambers, Ray Brown.

*Australopithecus robustus, Homo habilus, Homo sapiens.*

Launched like a dhow from Mombasa to the Bering Strait,

slurred like semantics in the big bands of Dave Holland and King Oliver,

walking from New Orleans to Chicago,

New York to Copenhagen.

Neils-Henning Orsted Pedersen and Charlie Haden.

Sino-Tibetan resolved to the patois of Ron Carter.

Spoken in Maa,

Maa, Mingus,

Mingus Maa, Mingus Ah

Mingus Ah Um.


Bent like the bowed horizon.

Devolved in dialects of arco and Proto-World.

Bracketed by Bird Calls and Pussy Cat Dues.

Formalized in flatted fifths and declensions of Malayalam.

Spoken in suffixes of syncopated sunsets.

The word in the root at the base of the tree where Mingus was born:

Mingus Ah

Ah, Ah

Mingus Ah

Mingus

Mingus

Mingus

Mingus Ah Um.

# BLUES FOR TRANE

*i*

*In the limit of form is love,*
*at the limit of form is love,*
*within the limit of form is love,*
*beyond the limit of form is love,*

*love caressing the summer field and the harmony of days,*
*love caressing the wound of loss and the sorrow of broken days,*
*love receiving the grace of love and the melody of days,*
*love embracing the devotion of love and surrender of restless days.*

John Coltrane blew the blues
and in his blues he blew
Jimmy Heath and Benny Golson
at the Woodbine Club on Twelfth and Master.

John Coltrane blew the blues
and in his blues he blew
Bird and Diz at the Five Spot.

John Coltrane composed chords, couplets, honks, compassion,
arpeggios, gospels, third-connected clusters,
broken rhythms, polyrhythms, improvised ostinatos,
multiphonics in prophesies of hailstorms and sonic waterfalls,
seraphic squeals, screeching epiphanies, sheets of sound.

John Coltrane composed High Point, Spruce Street, segregation in Alabama,

lyrical textures, modal conversations, pentatonic penetrations,

Giant Steps, revelations, codas in every key,

Blue Train, Coltrane, Soultrane, Chasin' the Trane.

Love, in the merciful wonder of knowledge.

Love, in the gracious resolution of God.

Love, Comes Love, No Greater Love, A Love Supreme.


*ii.*

In the voice of his horn,

Hamlet where he was born.


Hymns in the transcendent tone of an angel

probing the harmonic potential of time.


The resonant reduction of the blues.


On tour with Eddie Vinson,

in partnerships with Monk and Miles.


Phrases piercing the collective paradigm,

breaching the convention of consonant borders,

tempting the expressive appetite of energy.


In evolving languages of modulating motives,

in sacred vocabularies of mystic ciphers.

Pulsing daemonic convolution,

freedom is,

freedom is,


Freedom is love.

Freedom is harmony.

Freedom is love.

Freedom is beyond harmony, anti-jazz.


*iii.*

*At the limit of form is love,*

*in the limit of form is love,*

*around the limit of form is love,*

*outside the limit of form is love,*


*Love caressing the summer field and the laughter of unbroken days,*

*love caressing the rip of loss and the sorrow of broken days,*

*love receiving the redemption of love and the melody of days,*

*love embracing the desire of love and surrender of endless days.*


John Coltrane blew the blues

and in his blues he blew

Johnny Hodges and Dexter Gordon

Live at the Village Vanguard.


John Coltrane blew the blues

and in his blues he blew

Hawk and Pres.

John Coltrane divined cries, vamps, shrieks, lines at the tonal center,

autobiographical narrations, pentecostal punctuations,

incisive anguish, eruptive ecstasies, pianistic pilgrimages

to Dakar, Olé, Africa, India, Brasilia,

Ascension, Meditations, Interstellar Space.


John Coltrane divined choirs, squeaks, Huntington, sermons in every register,

incantatory constructs, sweeping structures, sliding sequences, universal signs,

tobacco sheds, Impressions, dance halls in Louisiana,

freedom in the discourse of tonic releases.

Love, in the furious discovery of spirit.

Love, in the relentless urgency of light.

Love, Just Love, No Greater Love, A Love Supreme.

# INTERVALS

*i*

She enters the club like cool water swirling over rocks.


Skin the color of cocoa carried by galleon from Ghana to Jamaica,

raised by the cane of sugar plantations,

red earth and tin roofs of Cornwall.

Eyes like quarter notes from the keyboard in the corner

of the band that swings to an Art Tatum tune,

while pool cues and darts flash like aspirations

in the chill of a hard winter's night.


She crosses the floor to a spot by the fire and lays her purse on a chair

as she removes a smooth coat like runnings of the Black River.

Half tones ripple from the keyboard in the corner—

roll to a Bud Powell tune

as plucked strings from a clavichord click in her head

like the wooden strips of an mbira,

sonatas of some eighteenth-century composer,

jacked heads of a harpsichord that snap

like the high notes on a Viennese piano,

Bach at the Thatched House,

Mozart at the Bavarian Court,

Thelonius Monk tripping at the Village Vanguard

on the mop stick hammers of a baby grand.

She orders whiskey and sits down.

There are arias blowing like headwinds of a cold front
keyed by Oscar Peterson on the night train,
there are gospels rising like a voice in the choir in the Church of the Ribbed
     Whale in Trelawny,
there is faith in the flight of arpeggios that soar like frigate gulls from the rafters
in the foyer,
ebonies and mahoganies like rondos and rubatos,
rigorous rivalry and the convolutions of counterpoint,

and a single candle in a tumbler on the table.

Mama said if you want more than rice and peas you have to leave this place,
cocoa and cane fields promise nothing to you.

*We were hunters of boar in the ancestral forest.*
*We were sculptors of thrones bearing magical masks.*
*We were fishermen braced by the grace of the sea.*

*ii*
New York takes its pleasure like an indifferent lover.
Its passionate suitors swell the pulse of its streets.

Past the sequined façades of success on Fifth Avenue,

by the towering billboards of grandeur on Broadway,

to the unpracticed pantomime of art in the Square.

She transposes Bleeker to the Blue Note on West Third,

grid of the city in the grip of her hand,

its symmetrical lanes like a harmonic ledger

transcribing the traffic of tugs on the Hudson,

scheduling her syllabus of studies Uptown,

melodic scales of the Lydian mode,

dynamic variation in the compositions of Ellington.


She pauses to reflect on the intervals of passage.


*Branded like bulls in the coastal stockades.*

*Shackled like convicts in the commerce of slave ships.*

*Auctioned like meat in the markets of port towns.*

*Free as Maroons in the province of mountains.*


And she recalls the rum shops and the dance halls of Kingston.

Rock steady and the rub of roots reggae.

Bob Marley on Third Street in Trench Town.

Beat of the breeze in the coconut palms.

The uncharted beaches from Negril to Long Bay.

Cocoa in her cup in her clapboard homestead in Hopeton, Jamaica,


and the flicker of ivory, cool water swirling over rocks.

# GLISSANDO

# HYMNS

Now that leaves

empty trees

and scatter my lawn

like splinters

of sunset,

I am wrong to think

their branches

point to nothing,

as if the sky

were nothing,

as if nothing

didn't matter,

as if only evergreens

have bearing,

bananas and coconuts

make sense;

I am wrong to think

the rebounding sea

or the bordering Potomac

signify more

than the sweet gum

graphed to a plot of stars,

or the red maple drawing

a range of light,

or the scrub pine

subscribing the moon.

I have been duped

by the conceiving sun:

clearings configure a

prolific canopy,

the setting sky is as

rich as ebony,

leaves soar like hymns

to the night.

# SPRING 1979

*i.*

Hands on the wheel of that battered Dodge pickup

heavy with lumber & scrap

on the narrow tar road through the hayfield

& ridge on the edge of Topsham to the dump.


Those early spring days when the coast

pulled its chill & the thick salt fields

lent the smell & look of growth to the day.


To the driver, with the purpose & privilege

of routing the labor of hands made rough

by hammers to the heap of progress of others.


Driving what was not needed to the refuse of what was.


*ii.*

How could he know that the husk of his body

held the seed of his destruction?


How could he see that the seed would grow like silence

through the synapse of his days?

Action composed achievement: Paris, London,

the sweep of the Danube & the Philharmonic.


In the opulent music, who could hear?

# APPLE

*cf. Blake*

The apple Adam ate glittered like the eye of God
in the sun-gathered garden of peaches and pears,
whitewater brooks and tumbling banks,
worms tunneling holes in the flesh
of the papayas and paw paws, pilis and pangans
in the orchard where fruit and the tree could be found.

*Red like the plumes of the bird in the sun,*
*fruit like the figs and the pomegranates there,*
*cooling and crisp like the olive and grape,*
*simple and smooth like the skin of the girl,*
*fragrant and lean like the leaves of the tree,*
*swaying to songs and the surge of the wind.*

The swinging sun swelled the dates and the days
in the perpetual orchard of persimmons and plums,
and sliding of worms in the festering fruit;
tasting of longing and love, he climbed down,
seeing the garden and woman at rest,
back to the earth in his shame and his pride.

# YOU KNEW THIS

*i.*

Even genetic memory

couldn't keep you from crying.


Or if your gills would work.


Nonetheless,

expanding, contracting,


your lungs, the Universe, the Act,


perpetuate the illusion.

Or shall we say, image.


Hail Plato! Hail Krishna!

Hail ancestral sea!


ii.

The flip side.


In 3-D!


iii.

You didn't know.

Each completion filled an absence.

Each conclusion forged a silence.

Your compulsion to create –
mix molecules, swap spit –
affirmed what your mind could not.


*iv.*
Still.

# HOLLERKÜCHLE

*The elder tree's healing powers are in its roots, leaves, blossoms and*

*berries.*

In Vancouver, you offered

a seat facing the bay,

salmon on our plates;

in Selçuk, we sampled

olives and cheese, watching

Agamemnon sail in;

Vienna, we jogged

the Volksprater

by the sausage vendors,

scarfed schnitzel under a tent,

you sent me *Original Badisch*

and I cooked potato soup

and Kratzede until,

in Berlin, on the Spree,

over asparagus and ham,

you told me he had made you Hollerküchle,

to heal the wounds.

[*Hollerküchle are elderberry fritters.]

# APPETITE

I want the woman cleaning fish by the wharf,

I want the girl in the Taquería.

At dinner, I want the belle serving rice and beans,

I want the looker grilling pike.

# ANDANTE

# DAY OF THE DEAD

*i*

The world is a toad floating among lilies.


Offer coffee, tequila, enchiladas, and chocolate.

Light candles, hang portraits, burn incense.

Spill the light of the day and the rain on the earth;

years are a bundle of reeds.


Return from the shadows, cross the new river,

set your altar with marigolds and lace.

Feast on pumpkins, grapes, rice and beans,

take your seat at the table


on the Day of the Dead.


*ii*

Wind that stirs the stars, blue and cold,

carry your loved ones home for the holidays.

Hold death as a mirror, be seen as you are:

bones, marionettes, cartoons, comics,

*calaveras*, coffins, masks,

pantomimes of importance in a traveling show,

illusions of substance in a transient stream,

skeletons, impresarios, tamales pounded from flesh.

Welcome back, freshen up,
on the Day of the Dead.

*iii*

Eat the bread of the dead, pick the flower of the dead,
dance the dance of the dead

on the Day of the Dead.

Drink mescal with the dead, camp out with the dead,
sing dirges with the dead

on the Day of the Dead.

Mariachi with the dead, laugh with the dead,
marry with the dead

on the Day of the Dead.

*iv*

Papel picados for the angelitos, All Saints Day,
*ring the bells that call you home.*
Sweets for the animas, All Souls Day,
*serve sugar skulls and wine.*

Offer coffee, tequila, enchiladas, and chocolate.

Light candles, hang portraits, burn incense.

Spill the light of the day and the rain on the earth;

years are a bundle of reeds.


Return from the shadows, cross the new river,

set your altar with marigolds and lace.

Feast on pumpkins, grapes, rice and beans,

take your seat at the table


on the Day of the Dead.

# U STREET STRUT

*Got the whole world swingin' to the rhythm of this music,*
*got the whole world dancin' to this syncopated beat,*
*got the city folks shakin' to the Big Bands on Black Broadway,*
*got the pretty boys struttin' to the clubs down on U Street.*

Jukin' 'n' jivin' to this music called jazz
in a club on the Black Broadway of soul.
She's hip to the strip and the razzamatazz
but don't know what the evening will hold.
It's got legs.
She's got class.
There are ghosts in her past,
yet there's nothin' but strut on the floor.
And her body is prayin' to the saxophone swayin'
and the bandleader callin' for more.

Drummer swings
lady sings,
he's got sticks,
she's got tricks,
he's got beat,
she's got heat,
she's got moves,
she's got grooves,
she's got dreams,

she's got schemes,

in control,

she's got soul.

        *I got Ella, I got Louis,*

        *I got Betty, I got Billie, I got Bessie, I got Pearl,*

        *got the Howard, got the Lincoln,*

        *got the Caverns, got the Gardens,*

        *got the Bali, got Cecelia's*

        *got the Poodle Dog Café.*

        *Around the corner in Little Harlem*

        *I got Dinah, I got Lena,*

        *I got Langston, I got Eubie, I got Benny, I got Nap*

        *Got the whole world swingin' to the rhythm of this music,*

        *got the whole world dancin' to this syncopated beat,*

        *got the city folks shakin' to the Big Bands on Black Broadway,*

        *got the pretty boys struttin' to the clubs down on U Street.*

Duke Ellington's band's in the club tonight

Cab Calloway's sippin' a beer,

Sarah Vaughan's under the weather tonight

and there's no one you'd rather hear,

but when she steps to the stage like a Yoruba Queen

and the woodwinds begin to sound,

from Thirteenth & U to Seventh & T

there's nothin' but Aretha around!

Keyboard swings,

lady sings,

he's got lines,

she's got time,

he's got keys,

she's got fees,

she's got class,

she's got sass,

she's got dreams,

she's got means,

in control,

she's got soul.

*I got Chi Chi's, I got Jo Jo's, I got Polly's, I got Nema's,*
*I got Twins, I got Sangham's, I got Ben's Chili Bowl,*
*I got U-Turn, got U-Topia, got the Island, got Negril,*
*got Tobago, Tropicana, got the Florida Avenue Grill.*

*Got the whole world swingin' to the rhythm of this music,*
*got the whole world dancin' to this syncopated beat,*
*got the city folks shakin' to the Big Bands on Black Broadway,*
*got the pretty boys struttin' to the clubs down on U Street.*

# RUBATO

# NOTHING, SOMETHING

*a.*

On this slip of time, neither here nor there,

Merely taking your next step.

you negotiate reversals.

The rest is semantics.

Ignorance becomes knowledge. Vacancy becomes visible.

Breakers at Bondi. Macaws in Manaus.

Silence absorbs the sound of this page.

*b.*

Nevertheless, in a language without lexicon,

Commerce. Love.

projecting scenes of unparalled symmetry,

In the silent art, *faith is everywhere.*

a binding energy propels.

You know because you are.

Not!

# MIKE'S DREAM

*for Mike Gillispie*

Smashed fifths from the flat on the flip side of the wall.

I press my ear.

Voices, odd intervals, retro.

Move the cabinet, the table, the TV.
Not the sugar of Sweet Sue, kiss of Perdido,
overdose of honey —

who is that cat slapping the keys?

From San Juan Hill in Harlem
to Minton's on One Hundred Eighteenth Street,

from Prohibition, crushed ninths,
stride, pump, slide, swing —

the Biblical simplicity,
the curve of sound.

*Monk's Dream, Monk's Mood, Monk's Point.*

I press my ear.

# SILK ROAD SUITE: THE MARKET SONG

*Spirit-wind spiraling through passages,*
*caravans cutting trails through desert sands,*
*camels moving merchants on the trade roads,*
*whisper tones unraveling like silk*

*Chang'an to the Imperial Court in Rome,*
*spirit-voices singing in the reeds,*
*artisans, caliphates and warriors*
*flutter-tonguing swallow-songs for silk*

Zhang Qian prisoner of Xiognu. Emissary of Emperor Wudi to the West.

Gaming bandits in the Gansu, antelopes, gazelles,

tribes abandonned by heaven, demons mounted on pigs,

tracking moving sands to the Jade Gate Pass through the Land of Death,

Hami, oases of Turfan and Kuqa,

on roped camels racked with musk, rubies, gunpowder, pearls,

apothecary, millet, persimmons, plums,

in caravans twisting like dragons, with no landmarks but bones,

from fields of summer wheat, packing porcelain and cinnamon

to purchase sacred horses poured from water,

Yuezhi trading flying horses for silk.

*Offer to the Goddess of Silkworms,*
*Fuxi and Nugua entwined,*
*mirror slips and satin robes*
*from the land of fish and rice*

*Soften the gum in the binding thread,*
*spin filaments like moon-lit trails*
*to the choraling wind in the mulberry leaves,*
*Silk Road in the cocoon*

Caravanserai in Kashgar. Crossroads to the West.
Fierce and impetuous, coarse merchants bargained
in the Great Bazaar for cotton, knives, carvings, glass
from carts, in street stalls, under wooden balconies,
behind wooden shutters, by narrow doorways,
at the base of the roof of the world,
with courtesans and warriors weary from walking,
with cameleers fitting horses and yaks for saddles and harnesses,
tendered  mutton, rhubarb, carrots, eggs,
anise, apricots, pots, pans,
piles of bread from bakers bent over brick ovens,
to skull-capped elders in noodle shops,
to silversmiths, bootmakers, menders, thieves
haggled at tea for carpets and sheep skins,
magicians and soothsayers embroidered like silk.

*Percussive wind, propelled from Kucha,*
*guide the trader on his journey to the plains*
*by flowing water, fragrant woods,*
*compel him like the siren in the flute*

*On waves of sand, through mountain passes*
*sustain him like the notes of minstrel songs*
*from bitter sandstorms, blinding cold,*
*in voices like the winding of the flute*

In the Great Domed Market of Samarkand,
merchants, acrobats, mathematicians, monks
exchanged cultures like coins, beads from Syria,
coral from Lebanon, fat-tailed sheep,
dancing boys from Merv,
by ostriches in the Plane Tree Garden,
peacocks in the Garden of Heart's Delight,
to  mosaics of astronomers mapping the stars,
peddled almanacs and amber, jasper, jet,
pomegranates, paper for the price of silk.

*Suspended between darkness and light,*
*aspara, mendicant on the path,*
*compose your mystic strand*
*in harmonics like the ashiq*

*From the wine-colored mountains of Persia*

*find scrolls in the grottos of faith,*

*in the pure sword of the spirit,*

*trail of the eight-fold way*


*For love of the one-eyed people,*

*for love of the oracle-bone,*

*for love of the nomadic kingdom,*

*for love of the terrible wind,*

*for love of the wild grass,*

*for love of the desert song,*

*for love of the city of shadows,*

*for love of the solace of silk*


Riches for the Silk People from the East.


For Romans to bear the fabric of light

nobiles traded the earth-born lambs,

lapis, ivory, lacquer, wool,

in palaces of crystal columns,

under mosques of turquoise tiles,

from woven mats, to camel bells,

by hawk and by falcon, by fluted reed,

for lust of knowing what should not be known,

for the hundred thousand fools of God,

for the transcendent touch of silk.

*Spirit-wind spiraling through passages,*
*caravans cutting trails through desert sands,*
*camels moving merchants on the trade roads,*
*whisper tones unraveling like silk*

*Chang'an to the Imperial Court in Rome,*
*spirit-voices singing in the reeds,*
*artisans, caliphates and warriors*
*flutter-tonguing swallow-songs for silk*

# LEGATO

# LOVE IS GRAVITY

In infinite variations
that do not change,
on spiraling levels
incalculably intertwined,

you take your next step.

Shape and color become you.

Landscape becomes you,
and reflection, and time.

You change. You tell a story.
There is no plot. You improvise.

Powder-white beaches. Palm trees.
Jealousy.

A spinning.

# APPEARANCES

*This is the message of the Wu Li Masters: not to confuse the type of dance*
*they are doing with the fact that they are dancing.*
*Gary Zukav,* The Dancing Wu Li Masters

1.

In the music of this place
color reveals absence.


As you reveal yours, by your presence.


Let's pretend. Take my hand.
Admire the blueberry field.
Crush a blueberry on your tongue.


Such sweetness cannot abide.


A sarabande. Then it's gone.


2.

But stay.

# The Homeowner

Regarding the combustion of oak

& the flaring of time & light

in the fireplace in the family room

matter measured in red shifts

diffused as the oxidation of order

a man adjusts his TV contemplates

fixing the thermostat raking

the leaves feeding the kids

while his couch deconstructs

& the shrub he would trim

appears only in contour & need &

the program of his life is already tuned in

# REDUCTO

The ideal poem contains ideal words

uttered in the ideal way

at the ideal time

by the ideal

one

# COASTAL BLUES

It was a cold night on the coast of Maine
when you taught me the blues.

I dreamed of falling.

Angels fell with me.

Rock rose from the earth like a canyon.

# PARALLEL

        runs a river.

Cascading toward me.

White-freckled, speaking.


*Watch them leap like salmon.*

*Watch them hide like trout.*


2.

*is what it is.*

*only what I see.*


b.

On the down side

rapids pursue, partner, propel.


d.

*The idea!*

# CORRESPONDENCE

Snow that phrases branches in winter

is the conversation of spring


Concurrence of blossom with ice


Repeated now in the gum and hickory

mute as the holly and laurel are green

# It Was So Cold I Had to Burn my Poetry to Survive

I had no other fuel -
snow fell in sheets.

I lit my Title Page,
incinerating my theme.

Twigs wouldn't take;
I ignited Acknowlegments,
searing assurance.

Copyright, Table of Contents -
identity and structure -
up in smoke.

To fan the blaze
I fed my notes, diffusing history.

I was cold. Desperately,
I torched my poems, one by one,
oxidizing substance.

When I had fried my last poem
night fell, I was freezing.

Frantically, I wrote,

on leaves, on bark, on my clothes.

Long poems, short poems,

metaphysical couplets - quickly consumed -

sonnets that burned hot and slow.

I was naked. Day broke.

# CODA

# Rainy Night in Old Town

Saxophone on a rainy night in Old Town,

bassist laying it down behind the groove.

The sun don't shine.

Dreams feel like summer, slide as runoff on the pane.

Time fades like lamplight, dims to shadows on the street.

Strangers reach for shelter from the chill.

But the keyboard signs,

the drummer plays.


Saxophone on a rainy night in Old Town,

keyboard laying it down behind the groove.

These are the measures,

notes spilling like autumn leaves,

harmonies that make the sidewalk bend like starlight through the fog.

Harmonica draws the southern breeze in swirling beads of color by the curb,

ambers, russets, yellows, blues,

the curling tones of soil and sky that rise and tumble back and forth like

      waves.

But the bassist walks,

the drummer plays.

Saxophone on a rainy night in Old Town,

drummer laying it down behind the groove.

Snares trip like cobblestones.

Ideas pulse like streams, ripple through the veins.

Strokes like wipers in the cold that drive the waterfront to flood,

wash like headlights in the mist,

brush the elms in modes of red,

while the keyboard kicks

and the drummer plays.


Saxophone on a rainy night in Old Town,

reedman laying it down behind the groove.

Bartender slinging shots like satin sheets.

With eyes that serve the soul's desire for more than easy scores and one-night

stands,

and passion plays that skip the mark,

hands that turn the knob for slipping friends.

A flute flutters in on lines like shoots of columbine in spring,

tapping remedies like wine,

dropping names like tears from cats.

In runs that raise the riverbed the way

the keyboard comps,

the drummer plays.


*Saxophone on a rainy night in Old Town,*

*bassist laying it down behind the groove.*

# Notes

"The Silent Art": Phrases refer to Wallace Stevens' "The Man with the Blue
   Guitar" and "Of Mere Being".

"Kyoto": Fushimi Inari is one of Japan's principal shrines dedicated to the
   Shinto god of agriculture, Inari, and his messenger fox, Kitsune. Fushimi
   Inari is remarkable for the thousands of red gates ("torii") arching the
   trail up Inari mountain. Shoren-in and Sanjusangen-do are ancient
   Buddhist temples of the Tendai school.

"Moving Pictures": *the best we can ever do is say that an electron has a
   particular probability of being found in any given location*
               *Brian Greene,* The Elegant Universe

"Location, Location": after W.S. Graham.

"Dreamtime": In Aboriginal legend, the Australian landscape is crisscrossed
   by trails of words and musical notes scattered by totemic ancestors.

"Pax Harmonica": A musician suggested that the tone of a harmonica is
   "wide."

"Double Bass": *Mingus Ah Um* is one of the seminal recordings in jazz. The
   poem references Peter Matthiessen's *The Tree Where Man Was Born*
   and John McWhorter's *The Power of Babel*.

"Intervals": The Maroons (from the Spanish word *cimarrón*) were a band of
    slaves who waged a rebellion in Clarendon Parish, Jamaica, in the late
    1600s.

"Apple": Based on William Blake's illustrations to John Milton's *Paradise Lost*.

"Hollerküchle": *In old myths, the elder tree ("Holunderbaum") was associated*
    *with Frau Holle (the spirit who watched over domesticity and household*
    *morals), and farmers used to doff their caps out of respect when they*
    *passed one.*
                        *Monika Graff, Heidi Knoblich,* Original Badisch

"U Street Strut": In the early 1900s, before the Harlem Renaissance, U Street
    in Washington, DC, anchored by the Howard Theatre, the Lincoln
    Theatre, and the Crystal Caverns, was the social and cultural capital of
    black America.

"Nothing, Something": *every particle has a corresponding antiparticle with*
    *the same mass but the opposite charge*
                        *Ian Smith,* Why Beauty is Truth

"Mike's Dream": Thelonius Monk (1917-1982), regarded as a founder of bebop,
    departed from conventional jazz with compositions and improvisations
    marked by dissonant harmonies and angular melodic twists, as well as
    an unorthodox, percussive approach to the piano. The phrase "overdose
    of honey" refers to flutist and saxophonist Eric Dolphy (1928-1964),
    who, unaware of being a diabetic, ingested large quantities of honey on a

European tour, which led to a deep coma from which he never recovered.

"Silk Road Suite": From approximately 200 BC to 1000 AD the overland trade
routes from Chang'an (Xi'an) to Rome were the principal conduits of
social, cultural, political, religious and economic exchange between East
and West.

"Appearances": Note that colors are reflections of light waves (or particles)
that are *not* present in an object; in effect, the color we see is the one
that's not there.

"Rainy Night in Old Town": Inspired by the jam session on Thursday nights
at Bistro Europa in Old Town, Alexandria, Va., during 2002-2003 led
by saxophonist Joshua Carr and featuring keyboardist Shep Williams,
bassist Andrew Cox, drummer Paul DeCastro, flutist Mike Gillispie,
and harmonicist Allen Holmes.

*Thanks*

Many of these poems were composed with music in mind. They have been
performed in clubs and cafés in the Washington, DC area with the Joshua
Carr Group, the Poesis group, and the Villainelles, in multiple variations.
Special thanks to Joshua Carr, Andrew Cox, Paul DeCastro, Mike Gillispie,
Allen Holmes, Aretha Grayson, James 'Curly' Robinson, and Shep Williams
for the inspiration.

# ABOUT THE AUTHOR

Clifford Bernier is the author of two poetry chapbooks, *Earth Suite*, *The Montserrat Review's Best Chapbook Summer 2010* and *Dark Berries*, one of The Montserrat Review's Best Books for Spring Reading 2010. He has appeared on the National Public Radio show "The Poet and the Poem from the Library of Congress." His poems appear in the *Potomac Review*, *The Baltimore Review*, the online journals *Notjustair* and *Innisfree*, and elsewhere, and he is featured on a CD of poetry duets, "Poetry in Black and White," as well as on two jazzpoetry CDs, "Live at IOTA Club and Cafe" and "Live at Bistro Europa." Founder and former host of the Washington, DC-area poetry reading series, Poesis, Bernier has been nominated for a Pushcart Prize and a Best of the Net Award.

# Also by Clifford Bernier

*Dark Berries*

*Earth Suite*

# More Poetry from Gival Press

*12: Sonnets for the Zodiac*

by John Gosslee; French translation by Elizabeth D. Watson, Spanish
translation by Jose M. Guerrero

ISBN 13: 978-1-928589-58-7, $15

"In John Gosslee's debut collection, *12*, he chisels to perfection sonnets that
masterfully treat the characters of the western zodiac…."
—*Carolyn Kreiter-Foronda, Poet Laureate of Virginia, 2006-2008*

*Adamah: Poème*

by Céline Zins; translation by Peter Schulman

ISBN 13: 978-1-928589-46-4, $15

2010 Honorable Mention—Paris Book Festival for Poetry
This bilingual (French/English) collection by an eminent French poet/
writer is adeptly translated in this premiere edition.

*Bones Washed With Wine: Flint Shards from Sussex and Bliss*

by Jeff Mann

ISBN 13: 978-1-928589-14-3, $15

Includes the 1999 Gival Press Poetry Award winning collection. Jeff Mann
is "a poet to treasure both for the wealth of his language and the generosity
of his spirit."
—Edward Falco, author of *Acid*

*Canciones para sola cuerda / Songs for a Single String*

*by Jesús Gardea; English translation by Robert L. Giron*

ISBN 13: 978-1-928589-09-9, $15

Finalist for the 2003 Violet Crown Book Award—Literary Prose & Poetry.
Love poems, with echoes of Neruda à la Mexicana, Gardea writes about the
primeval quest for the perfect woman.

*Dervish*

by Gerard Wozek

ISBN 13: 978-1-928589-11-2, $15

Winner of the 2000 Gival Press Poetry Award / Finalist for the 2002 Violet Crown Book Award—Literary Prose & Poetry.

"By jove, these poems shimmer."

—Gerry Gomez Pearlberg, author of *Mr. Bluebird*


*The Great Canopy*

by Paula Goldman

ISBN 13: 978-1-928589-31-0, $15

Winner of the 2004 Gival Press Poetry Award / 2006 Independent Publisher Book Award—Honorable Mention for Poetry

"Under this canopy we experience the physicality of the body through Goldman's wonderfully muscular verse as well the analytics of a mind that tackles the meaning of Orpheus or the notion of desire."

—Richard Jackson, author of *Half Lives*


*Honey*

by Richard Carr

ISBN 13: 978-1-928589-45-7, $15

Winner of the 2007 Gival Press Poetry Award / 2008 Finalist—ForeWord Magazine Book Award for Poetry

"*Honey* is a tour de force. Comprised of 100 electrifying microsonnets . . . The whole sequence creates a narrative that becomes, like the Hapax Legomenon, a form that occurs only once in a literature."

—Barbara Louise Ungar, author of *The Origin of the Milky Way*


*Let Orpheus Take Your Hand*

by George Klawitter

ISBN 13: 978-1-928589-16-7, $15

Winner of the 2001 Gival Press Poetry Award

A thought provoking work that mixes the spiritual with stealthy desire, with Orpheus leading us out of the pit.

*Metamorphosis of the Serpent God*

by Robert L. Giron

ISBN 13: 978-1-928589-07-5, $12

This collection "...embraces the past and the present, ethnic and sexual identity, themes both mythical and personal."
—*The Midwest Book Review*


*Museum of False Starts*

by Chip Livingston

ISBN 13: 978-1-928589-49-5, $15

Livingston - a "mixed blood" poet - presents a new approach to poetry through his experience.
"...Chip Livingston makes the ordinary exotic, erotic and extraordinary."
—Ai


*On the Altar of Greece*

by Donna J. Gelagotis Lee

ISBN 13: 978-1-92-8589-36-5, $15

Winner of the 2005 Gival Press Poetry Award / 2007 Eric Hoffer Book Award: Notable for Art Category
"...*On the Altar of Greece* is like a good travel guide: it transforms reader into visitor and nearly into resident. It takes the visitor to the authentic places that few tourists find, places delightful yet still surprising, safe yet unexpected...."
—by Simmons B. Buntin, editor of *Terrain.org Blog*


*On the Tongue*

by Jeff Mann

ISBN 13: 978-1-928589-35-8, $15

"...These poems are ...nothing short of extraordinary."
—Trebor Healey, author of *Sweet Son of Pan*

*The Nature Sonnets*

by Jill Williams

ISBN 13: 978-1-928589-10-5, $8⁹⁵

An innovative collection of sonnets that speaks to the cycle of nature and life, crafted with wit and clarity. "Refreshing and pleasing."
—Miles David Moore, author of *The Bears of Paris*

*The Origin of the Milky Way*

by Barbara Louise Ungar

ISBN 13: 978-1-928589-39-6, $15

Winner of the 2006 Gival Press Poetry Award / 2007 Adirondack Literary Award for the Best Book of Poetry / 2008 Eric Hoffer Award—Notable for Poetry / Silver 2008 Independent Publisher Book Award for Poetry
"…a fearless, unflinching collection about birth and motherhood, the transformation of bodies. Ungar's poems are honestly brutal, candidly tender. Their primal immediacy and intense intimacy are realized through her dazzling sense of craft. Ungar delivers a wonderful, sensuous, visceral poetry." —Denise Duhamel

*Poetic Voices Without Borders*

edited by Robert L. Giron

ISBN 13: 978-1-928589-30-3, $20

2006 Writer's Notes Magazine Book Award—Notable for Art / 2006 Independent Publisher Book Award—Honorable Mention for Anthology
An international anthology of poetry in English, French, and Spanish, including work by Grace Cavalieri, Jewell Gomez, Joy Harjo, Peter Klappert, Jaime Manrique, C.M. Mayo, E. Ethelbert Miller, Richard Peabody, Myra Sklarew and many others.

*Poetic Voices Without Borders 2*

    edited by Robert L. Giron

    ISBN 13: 978-1-928589-43-3, $20

    Winner 2009 National Best Book Award for Anthologies / Runner-Up 2009 London Book Festival Award for Poetry / 2009 San Francisco Book Festival—Honorable Mention for Poetry.
    Featuring poets Grace Cavalieri, Rita Dove, Dana Gioia, Joy Harjo, Peter Klappert, Philip Levine, Gloria Vando, and many other fine poets in English, French, and Spanish.

*Prosody in England and Elsewhere: A Comparative Approach*

    by Leonardo Malcovati

    ISBN 13: 978-1-928589-26-6, $20

    The perfect tool for the poet but written for a non-specialist audience.

*Protection*

    by Gregg Shapiro

    ISBN 13: 978-1-928589-41-9, $15

    "Gregg Shapiro's stunning debut marks the arrival of a new master poet on the scene. His work blows me away."
    —Greg Herren, author of *Mardi Gras Mambo*

*Psaltery and Serpentines*

    by Cecilia Martínez-Gil

    ISBN 13: 978-1-928589-52-5, $15

    Winner of the 2009 Gival Press Poetry Award / Runner-Up 2010 Los Angeles Book Festival Award for Poetry / Finalist 2010 National Best Book Award for Poetry / Finalist 2010 ForeWord Reviews Book of the Year Award for Poetry
    "This is a luscious and lustrous collection of poems..."
    — Gail Wronsky

*The Refugee*

by Vladimir Levchev

ISBN 13: 978-1-928589-57-0, $15

Translated from Bulgarian with Alicia Suskin and Henry Taylor.
"We are in the presence of a large spirit who writes in the greatest tradition of European masters."
— Grace Cavalieri


*Songs for the Spirit*

by Robert L. Giron

ISBN 13: 978-1-928589-08-2, $16$^{95}$

A psalter for the reader who is not religious but who is spiritually inclined.
"This is an extraordinary book."
—John Shelby Spong


*Sweet to Burn*

by Beverly Burch

ISBN 13: 978-1-928589-23-5, $15

Winner of the 2004 Lambda Literary Award for Lesbian Poetry / Winner of the 2003 Gival Press Poetry Award
"Novelistic in scope, but packing the emotional intensity of lyric poetry..."
— Eloise Klein Healy, author of *Passing*


*Tickets to a Closing Play*

by Janet I. Buck

ISBN 13: 978-1-928589-25-9, $15

Winner of the 2002 Gival Press Poetry Award
"...this rich and vibrant collection of poetry [is] not only serious and insightful, but a sheer delight to read."
—Jane Butkin Roth, editor of *We Used to Be Wives: Divorce Unveiled Through Poetry*

*Voyeur*
  by Rich Murphy

ISBN 13: 978-1-928589-48-8, $15

Winner of the 2008 Gival Press Poetry Award / Winner of the 2009 Los Angeles Book Festival Award for Poetry / Honorable Mention: 2009 London Book Festival for Poetry & 2009 New England Book Festival for Poetry "*Voyeur* is a work of vision and virtuosity. Concerned with relationships, marriage, sex and power, the poetry is dense, rapid, dazzling, the voice commanding, the speaker charismatic…spectacular."
—Richard Carr

*Where a Poet Ought Not / Où c'qui faut pas*
  by G. Tod Slone
  (in English and French)

ISBN 13: 978-1-928589-42-6, $15

Poems inspired by French poets Léo Ferré and François Villon and the Québec poet Raymond Lévesque in what Slone characterizes as a need to speak up. "In other words, a poet should speak the truth as he sees it and fight his damnedest to overcome all the forces encouraging not to."


For a list of poetry published by Gival Press,
please visit: *www.givalpress.com*

Books are available from BookMasters, Ingram, the Internet,
and other outlets.
or write

Gival Press, LLC
PO Box 3812
Arlington, VA 22203
703.351.0079

www.ingramcontent.com/pod-product-compliance
Lightning Source LLC
Chambersburg PA
CBHW020919090426
42736CB00008B/704